WITTENOOM

Mary Anne Butler

CURRENCY PRESS
The performing arts publisher

RED
STITCH

THE
ACTORS'
THEATRE

CURRENT THEATRE SERIES

First published in 2023
by Currency Press Pty Ltd,
PO Box 2287, Strawberry Hills, NSW, 2012, Australia
enquiries@currency.com.au
www.currency.com.au

in association with Red Stitch Actors' Theatre

Typeset by Brighton Gray for Currency Press.
Cover features Caroline Lee and Emily Goddard. Photo by Robert Blackburn.
Cover design by Mathias Johansson for Currency Press.

Currency Press acknowledges the Traditional Owners of the Country on which
we live and work. We pay our respects to all Aboriginal and Torres Strait
Islander Elders, past and present.

NATIONAL
LIBRARY
OF AUSTRALIA

A catalogue record for this
book is available from the
National Library of Australia

Contents

For my mum, Sally Rosemary Butler
And for Susie Dee, who helped nurse this script into the world

Foreword

The landscapes and colours around the Karijini gorges on the lands of the Banjima people are some of the most vibrant and unique on the planet. Vast gorges of crevassed red rock, green spinifex and saltbush, northern bluebells and purple Mulla Mullas, flowering wattles and acacias, trickles of sparkling creeks and deep green pools, and the ochre red sands over which sit the deep blue of the north western sky and the relentless yellow sun.

If you were one of the wedge-tailed eagles that soar and swirl in the thermals and currents above this land you might pick out thin blue lines that periodically appear and run through the red rock walls of the deep gorges. This is crocidolite—blue asbestos—and it is one of the most miraculous fibres on the planet. It doesn't burn. It is almost unbreakable. It resists acid.

Soar a little further and you will see below you holes in the rock wall and ruins of buildings clinging to the side of the gorge, and all around them, vast piles of blue grey rock cascading for hundreds of metres down the sides of the gorges. These are asbestos tailings—crushed rock mined by men in 36-inch stopes deep in the gorge walls, with bits of blue asbestos still attached to it, which weren't picked up by the suction in the asbestos mill that lifted the fibre from the crushed rock and conveyed it to fall down chutes where men looking like blue ghosts hammered the fibre into hessian sacks. The tailings were trucked up to the top of the gorge and dumped down the sides. The hessian sacks full of fibre stamped with the name Australian Blue Asbestos Ltd and the logo of the Colonial Sugar Refining Company (CSR) were piled onto trucks and carried out to the coast where they were loaded onto ships and sent around Australia and the world. Companies like James Hardie made a fortune from the products they made with asbestos fibre from Wittenoom, Baryulgil and Barraba in New South Wales, and from South Africa and Canada.

Soar on and you will pick out a single road running through the gorges out to a flat piece of land where you can see gridlines of what were the roads of a town where hundreds of people once lived and worked and played and died. This was Wittenoom. Now not even a ghost town, but an empty memorial to blind ambition and misplaced greed. A place where many who lived there found—for a short time— peace and happiness in the raw beauty, wide spaces and stunning colours of the land and sky. You might still pick out the blue tinge that runs through the red soil of the town and the white remnants of homes and buildings. And the shape of a racetrack on the edge of town where races were held once a year until not all that long ago. Where workers from the mine joined in the blue asbestos shovelling competitions and ran invitation sprints kicking up blue asbestos from the tailings that covered the track.

If it is the wet season you might see the Fortescue River surging through the gorges, the torrents picking up blue tailings and sending them down to the rock pools and sandy tree lined areas around them. You might see blue tailings deposited high up in the branches of the ghostly gums.

Wittenoom is a place of contradictions. A place of raw beauty but highly wrought devastation. A place where, when the mines operated between the 1940s and 1960s, working was as hard as it was possible to do for human beings, and a country town miles from anywhere where the nights were warm and still and where life could be fun and free. A town where there is no longer a town. A place of life and a place of death.

It is these contradictions which Mary Anne Butler exposes so painfully and so clearly in *Wittenoom*.

Because it is death that now infuses and illuminates the name and the memory of Wittenoom.

Because that miracle blue fibre is one of the deadliest natural things on the planet. If it gets into the lungs and the pleural spaces around them it can trigger off reactions that 20, 40, 60 years later turn into a cancer called mesothelioma. There is no cure for mesothelioma yet. It is one of the most devastating, debilitating, demeaning and painful diseases known. It kills most sufferers within twelve months, and the death is often agonising, literally breath-taking, terrible and shocking. It can also cause another lung disease called asbestosis which might also kill. And it can cause lung cancer.

And the terrible shocking truth that took many years and several pitched court battles to uncover was that from the start, CSR knew the dangers of asbestos—dangers which became ever more real and frightening over the years the mine operated—and it had not the will nor the inclination to do the things that were necessary to make the operations safer, and then would not confront the necessity to close the place down once it realised that the mines could not be made safe and that the folks who simply lived in the town were at risk as well.

Asbestos was used in Australia more than just about anywhere else in the world. James Hardie and CSR built fortunes on asbestos fibro building panels and asbestos lagging insulation. It was used in car brakes, sprayed insulation, beer filters, in valves and gaskets, as fire resistant clothing, in jewellery making, water pipes, in space heaters and as a backing for tiles in homes. And now Australia has one of the highest per capita rates of the deadly chest cancer mesothelioma in the world.

I was fortunate enough in the 1980s to be asked to join the battle to obtain justice for the victims of negligence and corporate disregard at Wittenoom, firstly by Robert Vojakovic and the wonderfully dedicated team at the Asbestos Diseases Society in Perth, who had come to the law firm I commenced with Taylor Smart to bring claims to court. Later, I worked with Peter Gordon and Jonathon Rothfield, brilliant and courageous lawyers, then of Slater & Gordon, who took over and ran three of the longest and most hard-fought trials in Australian legal history (Klaus Rabenalt v Midalco, Peter Heys & Tim Barrow v CSR, Simpson v Midalco, and a claim for a Point Samson wharf worker— Colin Watson) to establish precedents which led to the negotiation of a settlement of over 200 claims in the early 1990s. Peter and I took a team of lawyers and expert witnesses to Wittenoom at Easter 1987 and it was a trip I will never forget to a place I wish I could.

There were many heroes in that fight—Robert, Rosemarie and all at the ADS; Peter Gordon, Jonathon Rothfield, Luisa Dropulich, Sue Tait and the other lawyers at Slater & Gordon; the plaintiffs and their families who brought the claims, the barristers who represented the plaintiffs in court—David Ashley, Richard Stanley, Jack Rush, Daryl Williams, Roger Macknay, Chris Pullin, Rob O Connor and others; the doctors and medical witnesses who were prepared to give up days of their time to be grilled in court because of their dedication to their patients and their belief that they deserved better than to die in pain alone and without compensation—Bill Musk, Doug Henderson, Keith Shilkin, Bill Finucane, Gerry Ryan, Jim Leigh, Bruce Robinson, Cyril Minty, Nick de Klerk, Greg Deleuil and many others. And those that cared for the sufferers in the hospitals, such as Sue Morey and her team at Sir Charles Gairdner Hospital, including physicians Janet Elder, Bob Elphick, Martin Phillips, Tony Tribe, Alan James and Fiona Lake.

Two other groups of people need special praise and gratitude. First, two doctors who had, during the mine's operation, blown the whistle on the horrific conditions in which the men worked, and predicted the disease toll that would inevitably ensue, and who had been undermined by the mine management and ignored by CSR and those with governmental regulatory responsibility. Dr Eric Saint (later Professor Saint the founding professor at the UWA Medical School), a Flying Doctor, who, in 1948, told the mine managers and then wrote to the health department, that the conditions at the mine and mill would produce the 'richest and most lethal crop of asbestosis in the world's literature' (which was proved horrifically true) and Dr Jim McNulty (later WA Commissioner for Public Health), who went to Wittenoom as Mines Medical Officer in the 1950s to take x-rays and saw the beginnings of Eric Saint's prediction becoming real and who then diagnosed the first Wittenoom case of mesothelioma in 1960. He warned the CSR managers about the spreading of the blue asbestos tailings in the town to keep the red dust down, and was later horrified to see tailings being spread around the primary school playground. He got members of the medical establishment to harangue CSR's consultant company physician. But even after CSR suddenly closed the mine in December 1966 and sold it to Lang Hancock, asbestos tailings continued to be used for construction and dust abatement in the town into the 1970s. Both Eric Saint and Jim McNulty came to court in Perth and Melbourne and told their tales of tragedy and despair.

The other group were the people who lived and worked at Wittenoom and others who put their hands up to face the grilling of skilled barristers representing CSR—the workmates, the lower ranked managers, the people from the town—and others like the pilot, Richard Frith, who used to detect Wittenoom by the plume of dust from the mill. Barry Castleman and David Kilpatrick who knew the history of asbestos disease awareness, and Anne Batt who knew where the books were kept—those people who contacted us or were prepared to give evidence to help uncover the truth.

There were heroes in the media and academia too: Matt Peacock from the ABC who had fought a battle to raise awareness of the dangers and deadly consequences of asbestos in his radio program and book in the 1970s; Tim Hall who wrote a seminal article in *The Bulletin* magazine in 1974; Jock McCulloch who wrote a book *Asbestos: Its Human Cost*, exposing secrets of the Australian asbestos industry in the 1980s; Jan Mayman from *The Age*; Catherine Martin and Janet Fife-Yeomans from *The West Australian*; Paul Barry with his award winning *Four Corners* episode 'Blue Death'; Jim Gill of Nine's *Business Sunday* who was gifted secret internal files from CSR which told a lot more about what CSR had known than they had admitted in court, including the stunning exposition of CSR's brutal and contemptible litigation strategy—'They can die like flies but they will never pin anything on CSR', and Helen Dalley who grilled CSR MD Ian Burgess about it; Vicki Laurie of the ABC who kept the issue in the public eye; and Ben Hills who told the whole story in his book *Blue Murder*. Lenore Layman and Gail Phillips collect the history in their 2019 *Asbestos in Australia—From Boom to Dust*. And Kirsti Melville of ABC RN, who recently drew attention to the issues for the Banjima with her *Ghosts of Wittenoom* series.

And then the artists and writers who give us words to remind us of what it was all about and why we should never forget: Midnight Oil with 'Blue Sky Mine'; Alistair Hulett with 'Blue Murder' and 'He Fades Away'; Tim Winton in *Dirt Music*; and now Mary Anne Butler with *Wittenoom*.

Sadly, the litigation didn't end with the group settlement. Next came the claims for the residents and children of Wittenoom who contracted mesothelioma, then for the visitors and those who worked in the town or who stayed at Hamersley Iron's camp and lab set up in the 1970s. The mesotheliomas caused by that beautiful but deadly blue fibre, with latencies of 50, 60, or 70 years are still coming. It is estimated that one in every ten people who lived and worked at Wittenoom has died from, or will contract, fatal mesothelioma, a once rare disease and still one without a long-term cure.

There were also claims for some of the Banjima mob who had worked on the asbestos trucks or out at the jetty at Point Samson, or who were exposed to dumps in the gorges and at Roebourne—many of whom had contracted asbestosis and mesothelioma but who had been dying quietly on their lands.

And now the Banjima are fighting back. Having won in 2014, with lawyer Paul Sheiner, the native title fight for their lands in the gorges and Wittenoom, they are now fighting to have their lands made safe again for traditional activities like hunting and fishing—and living. I went back to Karijini in 2019 to meet with the elders—one with mesothelioma—and the land council, and to see again the stark beauty of their land and gorges.

Wittenoom has now been closed and almost entirely dismantled by the WA government. But the blue asbestos tailings still cover much of the land where the Banjima used to live and hunt. They have been pressing the government to remove or seal the deadly tailings so that their lands can be remediated. There have been some promises made but little real progress. The fight goes on.

As do the memories of those who were there.

Ms Butler's drama is hard reading if you know of the pain confronting the two protagonists. But there is a truth running through the pain like a seam of blue fibre through the orange rock walls of the Karijini gorges that is finally revealed. And like so often with great pain, great truth.

Like everyone, Dot, Pearl and Quinn are confined and perhaps condemned by things in life out of their control. But they want the same thing that most of us want—to make things better for their families. And perhaps a bit of justice.

John Gordon
Barrister, Douglas Menzies Chambers
September 2022

Wittenoom was first produced by Red Stitch Actors' Theatre at the Red Stitch Theatre, St Kilda, on 26 January, 2023, with the following cast:

DOT	Caroline Lee
PEARL	Emily Goddard

Director, Susie Dee
Set and Costume Design, Dann Barber
Lighting Design, Rachel Burke
Sound Design, Ian Moorhead
Stage Manager, Cassandra Fumi
Deputy Stage Manager, Georgina Bright
Assistant Lighting Design, Spencer Herd

Wittenoom was written under the development support of the Red Stitch INK program, Brown's Mart's Build-Up program, and an Australia Council Literature Board grant.

Special thanks to John Gordon for his Foreword.

CHARACTERS

DOT, an older woman.

PEARL, a younger woman.

SET / ERA

A hospital/hospice—The Present

Wittenoom, in Western Australia's remote Pilbara—The Past

NOTE

Characters segue between past and present, a 30-plus year time gap. This is not literal.

The playwright encourages cross-cultural casting in all her works.

Dot and Pearl are fictional characters. *Wittenoom* is a work of fiction, based on stories and public records of a mining town which operated in Western Australia's remote Pilbara.

This play text went to press before the end of rehearsals and may differ from the play as performed.

PEARL: The dogs of the apocalypse lie at her feet, ears alert.

    … waiting …

They can feel it in their flesh-bones; under their fur—
    sense the rising of the soul into the night
    as she floats, barely present;
    not quite ready
    to face the great emptiness.

Blue sickness gorging on her insides.
    Bones sucked empty of marrow.
    Flesh dissolved, eaten away.
    Her whole life drowning inside her own lungs.
    The hoarse rattle of death—not animal, not human.

The dogs of the apocalypse lie at her feet, fangs bared.
    They are patient. They can wait.
    They have waited for millennia.
    They understand that time melts glass, if you give it long enough:
    that flesh becomes ash,
    and ash becomes dust

    … eventually …

Breath shallow and rattling. Body all but corpse, now:
    bone-thin and hollow,
    skeletal sparrow.

Shudder of soul eclipsing—
    atoms reforming:
    soft,
    like stardust.

The dogs of the apocalypse rise
    tense
    curve their maws up towards the
    full

bright
moon.

Beat.

DOT: Pearl.
   PEARL!
   … there you are …
PEARL: She calls me Pearl, but I tell everyone I'm Saffron. Not orange
   and not red: an in-between colour like the rusted dirt of this country,
   before they laid the tailings.
DOT: Where you been? You're filthy. Now go wash up. We got a visitor.
PEARL: Another fella.
DOT: Miners, millers, stockmen, tourists. It's a smorgasbord out here.
PEARL: Smorgasbord of single men, looking for a wife.
DOT: Well, they can keep looking. Don't need a forever one, taking up
   space and time. Just need them for a night or two, so's to meet my
   needs—then on to the next when I feel the need again. Lonely out
   here, otherwise.
PEARL: What about me?
DOT: You're too young to be lonely. Teach you: you can be anything, all
   on your lonesome. Don't need someone else to make you a whole
   person. Now off you go. Me 'n' him got things to discuss. Not back
   until four, you understand?
PEARL: I cycle through the blue-grey streets, looking for other kids to
   play with. Past the pub, past the cinema, past the bakery, past the
   racecourse. Ride all the way out of town till I find the boys, surfing
   down a mountain of tailings, hessian sacks for surfboards. Get my
   own sack, run up to the top and surf down a giant blue wave.
   Again.
   Like I'm in the ocean; middle of the deep blue sea.
   Again.
   Feel free, and light, and strong. Like I can do anything.
   Again.
   Stack it at the bottom, all blue and bruised—but I don't care.
   Again.
   Again.
   Again.

Until the sacks are shredded by the sharpness of the tailings, so
we stop.

Light starts to fall across the ranges: yellow-gold-orange-red.
    Shadows grow bone-thin and fragile.
DOT: A cough. Dry. Persistent.
PEARL: Light fades beneath rock.
DOT: Then a hack. Can't stop.
PEARL: Here, at end of land's end
DOT: Phlegm and bile and raging chest.
PEARL: drowning in swathes of bones
DOT: …hard…
PEARL: where ghosts sing back their mournful songs
DOT: … to …
PEARL: through layers of crusted time
DOT: … breathe.
    Beat.

Have nightmares about fingers of poison spreading vivid across my
lungs; worming their way deep down into my chest.
    Wake up scared and shaking; lump of worry twisted low inside—

… and then …

bright
    red
    thick.
    Deep flecks of raw, fresh blood splayed out
    across the whiteness of my handkerchief
    in the shape
    of a star.
    Beat.

PEARL: Race Day, and in they come …
DOT: … chartered flights and motorbikes, four-wheel drives and utes,
caravans and Kombis …
PEARL: … churning up dust like slow-falling snow.
DOT: Ladies from Roebourne, Onslow, Carnarvon, Port Hedland strut
the blue-paved streets, fascinators quivering.

PEARL: They even come in from Perth. The Big Smoke.

DOT: Watch them goggle at the wild beauty of this place: blue skies and spinifex, ghost gums and budgies, roos and galahs, dingos and wildflowers.

Beat.

Well; will you look at that!

PEARL: ... she means the men ...

DOT: Bushies and townies, stockmen and wharfies, builders and labourers; all suited up

PEARL: in the forty-degree heat.

DOT: Sweating, and rugged, and handsome. Fresh meat in town tonight. Look at that one! Yeee-ha!

PEARL: Full-on cowboy rig; right down to the spurs.

DOT: Lean jaw and built chest. Arms that strong you could swing on 'em.

PEARL: ... and she does ...

DOT: The pub swells to five times its size and the campground splays out, spilling into the paddock next door. The front lawns of houses grow tents and caravans, swags and tarpaulins. Men sleep out under the open stars with only their coats for comfort.

PEARL: Mum puts a sign out on the front lawn advertising 'Camping', and three fellas pull in to set up amongst the dry blue tailings of lawn while she fusses and flutters and flirts about, joining them for a 'sundowner' while the sun's still high in the sky.

DOT: Pearl! Come on, we'll be late!

PEARL: At the track the bookies wave their tickets about, crowded in by punters who push forward, laying bets before the race starts. One fella bickers about who's next and someone bickers back and a fight breaks out; the two of them rolling in the dust: landing punches, ripping shirts, fists flying hard and fast and by the time they're done it's too late, the bookie's shut up shop and the race is about to start.

DOT: ... and they're off! Golden Dream won't leave her gate, and Blue Sky Mine throws his jockey right at the start. The rest of them gallop around the track while the medics carry the screaming jockey off, leg twisted at all the wrong angles.

PEARL: Dust kicks up around the track: whirlpool-whirring, spinning a blue-grey cloud around us.

DOT *dances in the whirling dust, joyous and unfettered.*

She puts her hand out for PEARL *to join her.*

Mum! Don't! You're embarrassing!

DOT: … you need to loosen up, girl …

PEARL: You got no shame!

DOT: … and it's Blue Sky Mine by a nose: unhindered by the weight of his jockey, running free as the wind.

PEARL: After the horses there's ice-cream and sack races.

DOT: Beer and Two-up.

PEARL: Tennis and golf.

DOT: Picnics, and swimming, and then—

BOTH: The Wittenoom Ball!

PEARL: All dressed up like peacocks and penguins.

DOT: Flirting and laughing and dancing and wine.

My dress is blood-red.

PEARL: Where'd you get that?

DOT: Made it myself, from curtains I found at the back of the pub. Coupla holes in them, but—

easily fixed.

Sprig of wattle in my hair. Each little flower like a tiny sun, exploding.

One fella grabs me around the waist and pulls me hard into him and we twirl and spin so fast we become a whirling cloud of hope. God, we dance. Until my feet go red-raw with it; layers of skin peeling off inside my shoes. And still we don't stop.

He asks me my name and I tell him it's Patsy, even though it's really Dot. Dot is a speck on the landscape; a nothing. Patsy has class— like Patsy Cline. That's the thing about way out here. You can be anyone; anything in this centre of the second chance.

They kick us out and we stagger up to the top of Mount Watkins: watch the stars pin-prick their way out from the inky black, making a pattern of possibility.

He peels off my dress and we have each other, slow and soft against the cool of midnight rock

PEARL: Biopsies.

DOT: until the birds start their happy cackling

PEARL: MRIs.

DOT: and glorious day peels itself upwards

PEARL: CAT scans.

DOT: from deep beneath the blood-red mountain ranges.

PEARL: PET scans.

DOT: A shadow. On my lung. Blue.

PEARL: Spread out in a river system: tributaries winding in and out and over and under; dense and dark and knitted and complex.

> *Beat.*

They'll fix it.

DOT: What if they can't?

What if it sets in and rots. Spreads and consumes me. Eats away at my body.

What if they can't get to it, can't—

eliminate it.

… what then … ?

> *Beat.*

PEARL: You look pretty.

DOT: I'm off to the pub.

PEARL: Again?

DOT: The government workers are here. They got some class, that lot. Who knows who I might meet?

PEARL: And bring home.

DOT: I shut the door.

PEARL: I can still hear you.

DOT: Well plug up your ears if you don't like it. A woman's got to have her exercise, otherwise she'd get all tight and stiff.

> *Beat.*

Your dinner's in the oven.

> *Beat.*

PEARL: Mum?

DOT: What?

PEARL: Who's my dad?

DOT: Don't know, don't care. Don't need a permanent man putting himself first. Just need you. The other half of me. My baby. My Pearl.

Call you Pearl because you're round, and shiny, and perfect inside my belly.

Don't care how you come out, either. Pearls can be any colour they want.

PEARL: You don't get teased at school. Called a bastard, called a—

DOT: Teach you to toughen up, let it wash off you like water off a shell. Learn early on: if you laugh in their faces there's nothing they can do back. Teach you to whoop, howl, dance, spin into the fullness of life. To live the world as lightly as you can. There's enough heaviness already, don't need to add to it from your own insides.

PEARL: I make myself a tomboy: cut off my hair, run like them, smoke like them, swear like them, ride bikes like them. Surf the wild rapids through the gorges in wet season, arse plugged into an inner tube, sliding, slipping, spilling out into the freedom of light.

Out in the bush they let me into their gang like I'm one of them, but in town they leave me on the outside; so I hover. Learn to live between worlds, like a ghost. Learn to live inside myself.

I like it in here, where I can be me. It's an in-between space.

It's my place.

Beat.

DOT: Sit at the counter where the government workers are standing. Pick out the tall one with the piercing eyes. Suave; like he'd be a Russian spy or a police detective in another life.

They invite me into their circle. Cross one ankle over the other—delicate—so's he can see the fullness of my legs. The ripeness. The ready-for-you shape of them. Joke a bit, laugh a bit, drink a bit, flirt a bit.

After dinner we dance on the endless verandah with the radiogram turned up as loud as it can go; wooden floorboards bending and shaking so hard that the needle keeps jumping from one track to the next. We drink The Fortescue dry that night. Roll onto the mattress in his room upstairs. Fuck all night like animals; wild and free.

See the pale white band of flesh around his ring finger in the new light of morning. Feel a sinking inside me. Maybe coz I thought this one was different.

This one felt solid
and real
and whole.

… I always see more in them than there really is …

Peel out of bed and slip on my dress. Carry my shoes and stockings
to the door, slide it open and slither outside, down the steps. Skate
back home before my alarm rings for work, and wakes up my shiny
Pearl.

    Beat.

PEARL: Wait two weeks for an appointment—finally get a fifteen-
minute slot. Walk into a small, airless room in a grey concrete
building.

DOT: The man sits behind his desk:
    black suit
    white shirt
    blue tie
    glasses
    long, thin hands.

PEARL: Delicate. The type you want in a surgeon.

DOT: Better than buff-bumbling bucket hands, anyway.

Watch sunlight pierce the glass paper weight on his desk:
    Round like a brain.
    Round like the world.
    Dust motes dance happy around it,
    mocking me.

He clears his throat. Hasn't looked at me once, not since we came
in the room.
    Hasn't looked up from his computer.
    He stays focused on it now, massive screen between us,
protecting him from me
    —or me from him.
    He reads from his screen: mesothelioma, he says. All through
your lungs.

My insides go cold. He keeps reading:
Stage Three.

Beat.

It's everywhere.

Beat.

Three months, he says.
Just like that.

PEARL: Hole deep inside where the wind whistles through.

DOT: Sorry?
Three months, he repeats.

PEARL: Holes beneath the bridge of reason.

DOT: Three months what?
Left. To live.
What?

PEARL: All the stars extinguished.

DOT: What about treatment?

PEARL: Birds falling from the skies.

DOT: It's mesothelioma, he says. There is no treatment.
No treatment?
No treatment.
You can get a second opinion, he says, but it won't change these results.
Then he's over. Done. Finished. Switched off and prepping for his next victim.

… and I am dismissed …

PEARL: The world moves in slow motion. Limbs weighed, and sluggish.
The ache of emptiness. The weight of a space.
The whole world stripped back to empty skin and bone.

DOT: Who the fuck are you anyway?

PEARL: Mum?

DOT: I mean; who the fuck do you think you are?

PEARL: Mum!

DOT: You're not a fucking prophet are you? Or a—a—a—
—what do you call them? Pearl! What do you call them?!

PEARL: … ?

DOT: Those Greeks who see into the future.

PEARL: Oracles.

DOT: You're not a fucking Oracle, are you? You're nothing but an overtrained monkey.

PEARL: Mum!

DOT: How can there be no cure? There're cures for cancer and typhoid and polio. How can this be bigger than any of them?

PEARL: Enough!

DOT: Fuck you. Arrogant twat.

PEARL: It's not his fault!

DOT: No-one tells me when to die. D'you understand? Not him. Not you. Not anyone.

PEARL: Okay! Enough! We'll get a second opinion.

DOT: Damn tootin' we will.

　　… arrogant fucking twat …

　　Long beat.

PEARL: I hate it at school, coz I don't belong. I'm not like the good kids up the front who answer all the questions right, and I'm not like the bad kids down the back who pass notes and flick rubber bands. I'm somewhere in the middle.

　　So I leave. Get a job in the miner's mess, with my mum. Watch them fumble, stumble their way out of the gaping maw of the mine when the shift horn sounds; blind-blinking moles folded in half by bending for eight hours straight in those tight dark stopes, only three feet high. They stagger in still coated in dust; clothes an inch thick with it. Blue hair, blue hands, blue faces. Serve them up their breakfast-lunch-dinner; who knows what meal it is to them, being down there in the dark so long. Crawling in after double shifts, fuggy and disoriented. Serve them up their King Brown beers, and clear the plates when they're done.

DOT: Some bloke slaps her arse, so I spit in his spaghetti. While he's still eating it.

　　Oy! Do that again, and I'll shit in it. She's fifteen. Touch her and you're dead. Understand?

　　He does.

PEARL: Feel worse for the millers, who crawl in like grey ghosts: asbestos dust in their eyes, ears, noses, mouths. Pulverising rock inside a cloud of dust so thick that even the overhead floodlights can't cut through it. Hands red-raw from peeling fibres out of the blue chunks that the miners bring up. Packing the fibres, sharp like needles into hessian sacks, using only their bare hands.

The only ones I never see are the Countrymen. The Banyjima mob. They don't get to eat in here. Management give the worst of the jobs to them: hurling the sacks onto the asbestos trucks, sitting on top of the sacks in full sun all the dusty, bumpy way out to Point Samson.

Feels wrong.

… everything feels wrong …

DOT: A young bloke gets diagnosed with asbestosis and takes his life before his time.

Don't wanna go through that, he tells his mum before she finds him, hanging from a high tree over Wittenoom Gorge.

PEARL: Out here the world stops dead, and you can hear your own thoughts.

Beat.

Out here, the world stops. Dead.

Long beat.

DOT: I always wanted a tattoo. Not quite like this. A panther, maybe. Fangs breaching up between my breasts; muscles chiselled and fierce, grasping life between its jaws. Or the Tree of Life; four hundred years old, in the middle of the desert. No sign of water, nothing else nearby. Just it, on its lonesome.

A tree which is older than I could ever hope to be.

I wonder what it thinks, that tree. When the sun strikes hard. When the rains still won't come. When it stretches its roots deep, deep underground; sucking for water. Sucking for life, and somehow finding it.

But I get a dot-to-dot tattoo. The cartography of cancer. The stops on this journey:

here

and here
and here.
Map of hope, etched in skin ...

... and if I follow it, perhaps it will take me to the place
where I can begin
again.

Beat.

PEARL: Mum starts doing shifts at the pub.

DOT: Might as well get paid while I'm checking out the fellas. Have my sly drink going on under the counter, but no-one seems to mind—as long as I'm fast, and friendly.

One night more government workers come in, but the tall suave one isn't there; it's the other mob. Medical officers with their travelling x-ray machine and a new thingamabob to measure the dust particles. There's an English fella and an Irish one, McNulty. He's handsome. Kind eyes. Wouldn't mind getting lucky with *him*, if the occasion arose ...

They sit in the dining room, and I head in for their orders. Take my time wiping down their table. Perk up my ears:

Appalling, the Pom says. Dire conditions. Dust and death and darkness. Did you see their safety gear? All brand new, issued for our visit, no doubt. Packed away again as soon as we leave.

They won't wear it anyway, says the McNulty fella. Underground, in that heat? It's hard enough breathing as is.

Readings in the Mill are through the roof, says the Pom—and half of them are refusing the chest x-rays. It's like they don't want to know the truth of it.

No, I say in my head. They don't. Because even though we know they're trying to help us, this is the best paying job any of us ever had, and we're scared. Scared to lose it. Scared to let this one little fibre of hope go; this once-in-a-lifetime opportunity to work our arses off for a few hard years so's we can save up a nest egg, pay off our debts, get our teeth fixed, buy ourselves a house in the city, give our children an education, retire to a lifestyle where we don't have to eat dog food every day in order to get by. All the things you lot take for granted.

But it stays in my head, because how do you explain a fear of poverty to the likes of them?

… so I finish my wiping …
PEARL: Slice open for extraction
DOT: … and I take their orders …
PEARL: cauliflower of cancer
DOT: … and I walk away.
PEARL: tumour like a taproot, twisted deep.
DOT: Hard to scrape
    all of it
    out.
PEARL: Sew her back together like a baseball: thin lines of red-raw.
DOT: So neat. So small.
PEARL: Threads too frail to hold a whole life together.
DOT: … and then …
PEARL: Eight rounds of chemo, each worse than the last. Veins, a network of lifeblood:
    pumping
    pulsing
    powering poison through her, in a race for the kill-off.
    Sneaky, duplicitous, multiplying cells. Two good cells die for every bad one.
DOT: Never been a gambler—yet here I am betting weeks, days, hours of my present for a future which may never arrive.
PEARL: Scalp like patchwork.
DOT: Veins itching; burning.
PEARL: Bruises that won't heal.
    But still she manages to cling on to these
    tiny
    floating
    fibres
    of hope.
DOT: Got to fight it. Got to try, but—
    Tired. So, so tired.
    Scared.

    Beat.

PEARL: What's that?

DOT: A wall.

PEARL: … more like a partition …

DOT: A partition, then. Who cares what it's called?

PEARL: What's it for?

DOT: I'm getting boarders in.

PEARL: What? Why??

DOT: Nonna down the road there's doing it. Put a sign up at the single men's quarters, now she's got seven of them in, each paying thirty-five shillings a week.

PEARL: You're going to bring seven single men in here?!

DOT: … one for every day of the week …

PEARL: Mum!!

DOT: … just kidding …

PEARL: Not funny.

DOT: What she gets from them covers the food and rent for her and her four kids—plus that no-good gambling husband of hers. She sends all his wages to the bank, and they've nearly paid their house off.

PEARL: Well you're not touching my room.

DOT: No, Princess. I'm not. But you will be helping me with the cooking. And the cleaning. And the washing. And the mending.

PEARL: I'm not washing any man's clothes.

DOT: Well I can't do it all on my own.

> *Beat.*

Come on, Pearl. Means we can start thinking of buying a place. In Cottesloe, even. Imagine that! Worth a bit of sacrifice now, to buy that kind of future.

> *Beat.*

PEARL: Only if I get power of veto.

DOT: What's that?

PEARL: It means I get to say who does and doesn't come in.

DOT: … dictionary on legs, you are …

> *Beat.*

PEARL: Watch her body convert matter into non-matter

DOT: Some nights I can hear them, deep inside me:

PEARL: gaunt fifty kilos falling backwards and counting:
DOT: the tiny remains doubling; tripling
PEARL: forty-nine
DOT: feeding on their own will.
PEARL: forty-eight
DOT: Cells multiplying:
PEARL: forty-seven
DOT: brewing
PEARL: forty-six
DOT: festering
PEARL: forty-five
DOT: swelling.
PEARL: forty-four.

> Bucket-by-the-bedside-bile; thin and green; acidic.
> Burning her oesophagus as it rises up through throat, mouth, teeth, lips.

DOT: Feel my dreams fall out of my chest and onto the floor.

> Watch them flap and flicker, evaporate into dust.
> Try to scoop them up and shove them back in, but—
> they don't fit any more. My chest has shrunk.
> Feel my wounds close over
> into nothing
> but
> silence.

> *Beat.*

PEARL: Me 'n' Mum go down to put a sign up at the single men's quarters.
> … is this where they actually live … ?
DOT: That's why they want to get out into a real home.
PEARL: There's no furniture. No bathroom.
DOT: … that shed out there, that's where they …
PEARL: No kitchen, or lounge room, or—
> nothing. Just eight beds crammed into a shed half the size of our place. Wooden boxes for shelves.
DOT: Stinks of old socks and undies.
PEARL: Old Greek bloke comes past. He's thin, and muscly: skin brown and leathered; wizened by the sun.

Looks at our sign. Looks at Mum. Looks at me.

Yes, he says. Just

—yes.

DOT: What's your name?

PEARL: Quinn.

He looks around the dormitory.

They call this death row, he says. But in here, your spirit dies long before your body does. He's got sad eyes; like he's seen things he shouldn't.

DOT: I wanted younger fellas.

PEARL: You wanted someone to help fix things around the place. Look how muscly he is.

DOT: Too thin. I like a man with some meat on him.

PEARL: We're not eating him, Mum. We're—

DOT: … well *you* might not be, but—

PEARL: Anyway; I have power of veto.

Beat.

It's yours if you want it. There's a shared room for sleeping—or the verandah, if you want your own space.

DOT: It's thirty-five shillings a week, paid on a Friday. All meals including your crib to take to the mine, and your washing done. Mending is extra. Shared living area and kitchen, and you respect the place, or you're out. Drinking in moderation only, and you pay for any damages. You keep your area clean and tidy, and you keep your eyes and hands well off my daughter.

PEARL: He moves in; chooses the verandah. Sets up a mozzie net over his bed. Gets a stained old lounge chair from somewhere. Covers it with a sheet to cheer it up a bit. Sits and rolls a cigarette and looks out to the range as the sun sets; a deep glow of happiness on his face.

Three other fellas turn up the next day, and we take two of them. The third won't stop looking at my breasts, so—

DOT: Piss off. We're full.

PEARL: Quinn has a Greek mate who comes and charms the pants off Mum—so he makes up the fourth.

DOT: Two Greeks, two I-ties. It's like the United bloody Nations around here.

PEARL: The Italians are young; barely eighteen.

DOT: … missing their mums …

PEARL: Quinn keeps them in line. Organises hunting parties. Brings back kangaroo and the odd rogue cattle they've found wandering away from the rest.

DOT: … the stockmen won't miss one or two …

PEARL: Makes us kleftiko, in the earth, like it should be made. And keftethes. And moussaka, when he can get the eggplants.

The young fellas make Mum a chicken coop out of 'borrowed' timber and fence posts, so we can have fresh eggs every day.

DOT: On Sundays if they're not on shift we all head out to the gorge; swing wild on the Tarzan rope. Hang high above the iridescent blue water

drop

down

down

down—free, and weightless

into deep, cold pools of possibility.

PEARL: I look up at the rocks, looming over us. The ranges, hemming us in. The hot, wet blanket of heat suffocating limbs, heart, brain. Feel small, and closed, and …

trapped.

But when I sit with Quinn and look out over the golden horizon to a place beyond us, it smells of something bigger, and better, and—

different.

Beat.

DOT: Tits thin, and drooping.

PEARL: We need to go alternative.

DOT: I had great tits, once.

PEARL: How about this?

DOT: Massive.

PEARL: Vitamin C shots.

DOT: Mountainous.

PEARL: Builds immunity.

DOT: But now? Not a woman, any more.
Not anything, any more.
Dry. Empty.
Veins void, and brittle. Nurse can't find the entry point. She stabs
—and stabs
—and stabs, but—
nothing.
Makes me drink two cups of water, then wait …
… and wait …
… and …

PEARL: There she is!

DOT: Takes half an hour for the infusion, by which point my bladder's
bursting at the seams, piss starting to sneak out. Try to hold it in, but—

PEARL: Ekes out onto the protective white paper. Seepage of dark, dank
yellow.

DOT: I beg and beg, but she orders me to stay. Tells me the vitamins
won't work unless I have the full dose. Tells me she won't be
reinserting the canula into *that* barren arm. Tells me it's not a
moveable drip, and just to hang on.

… agony …

Finally the bag empties, and she removes the canula. Bolt to the
bathroom:
piss
piss
piss.

Christ.

No-one warns you about the loss of dignity.

… nobody mentions that …

Beat.

PEARL: Quinn takes a shine to me. Not in a weird way, just … like a
grandpa. Tells me if I'm not gonna go to school then I have to read.

DOT: Why're you spending so much time with him?

PEARL: He gives me books.

DOT: What kind of books?

PEARL: Greek myths and legends. Gods and goddesses. Sirens and harpies. Gorgons and satyrs.

DOT: Oh. Not romance, then?

PEARL: No, Mum. Not romance.

DOT: … that's a shame …

PEARL: I ask Quinn if the stories are true, and he shrugs.

Truth is what you want it to be.

Beat.

These stories are lessons for life, he says. This mining company, it is King of the Underworld. Like Hades, they make sure their guests can never leave—but instead of a three-headed dog they have two-faced lackeys by their side. And the miners are like Pandora. There are evils flying all around them: dust, heat, flies and lies—but at the very bottom of all this is money, and money means hope. It is why we are all here. Greeks, Italians, Poles. Even the bloody Austrians have come. We leave our beautiful countries and the safety of family to come to this shithole.

Says he won't stay much longer, he's worried about the asbestos. Says he can't leave yet though, too many people back home depend on him buying them a proper future. Says he can hang on for another year, maybe two.

Beat.

DOT: Homeopathy?

PEARL: … it's when you …

DOT: I know what it is. Nutbars, all of them.

PEARL: Okay, then. Acupuncture.

DOT: Stick you full of pins? Double nutbars. Besides, these veins aren't up to any more of that business.

PEARL: Autophagy?

DOT: What's that?

PEARL: Water fasting. The body devours itself in an act of cellular cannibalism. Eats up its own bad cells.

DOT: Just by drinking water? Who *are* these people?

PEARL: Come on, Mum. Give it a go.

DOT: How much?

PEARL: Two thousand dollars.

DOT: For one week?

PEARL: You don't have to go there. Do it yourself. At home. Start with a short one. Forty-eight hours. Have an early dinner, get to bed, and when you wake up—bam, you're already twelve hours in.

Skip the next day's meals.

DOT: … nothing but water …

PEARL: … and the next …

DOT: Beer's ninety-five per cent water—

PEARL: Then that night you can have what you damn well want. Chips. Wine. Chocolate. Have a fried frickin' banana, if you feel like it.

DOT: And that's gonna cure this mesothelioma, is it? Maybe you should let the doctors know you've found a cure for the incurable. Just drink water! It's magic!

PEARL: Please, Mum. What if it works?

DOT: I make it to five hours. Four seconds to midnight.

Pour myself a thick glass of red, crack open the chocolate.

Feel them slide happy down my throat.

Make popcorn. Watch comedy on late night telly until I wee myself laughing.

Crawl into bed at four a.m., happy as a clam.

Fasting, my arse. My body knows what it wants.

Beat.

PEARL: I can hear Quinn yelling from a hundred yards away: Enough! I have had enough! They say they will drill air holes into the stopes, but they do nothing! They promise to fix the extractor fans, but they do nothing. Nothing! We are like moles shoved underground, stinking in the heat and choking on the dust. And everyone here is too scared to speak; too weak to complain, because their job will be given to one of the hundred others who are hungry enough to take such shitting work.

It is crazy, he says. This place is crazy. But the only way out from here is by plane, or private car. No-one can afford the plane ticket, and who here has a car? So we are trapped until we finish our contract. Trapped in this place where two years of this sentence takes ten years off your life.

Beat.

DOT: Lungs.
PEARL: I am tired, he says.
DOT: Spine.
PEARL: I am so, so tired.
DOT: Brain.
PEARL: … I want to go home …
DOT: Jesus.

… although it's a bit late for that, I suppose. He'd know I was hedging my bets.

Try to think positive thoughts. Make a list of all the good things:
wine
beer
chocolate
flowers
coffee
dogs
dresses
dancing

sex

My beautiful, shiny Pearl …

… but when I lie alone at night, the sleeping giants wake me
nudge me sideways
roll me out of bed
spin me into the cold black vortex
hurl at me their questions:
What if death is an endless aloneness?
What if it's eternal nothingness, but you have to stay there forever?
What if there are others down there who have died of sadness, sorrow thick on their skin as they barrel forward, foul-breathed, clamouring for new meat?
In my head I hear the echo of their losses: wild, like wolves, as they drop
down
down

down
howling
into the abyss.

Beat.

PEARL: Quinn gets sick deep in his chest: cough-cough-coughing till it hurts; hacking up his ribs, hawking small pieces of lung out from between his lips. Doctor here says it's too sudden for asbestosis, it's more like tuberculosis—so we move him into my room to keep the others safe, and set up a swag in Mum's room for me.

Gets so he can't walk more than three steps without having to sit down; lungs so caved in that his breath drags in sharp, like daggers. I bathe him, toilet him, try to sponge the sickness away—but he fades to a shadow and slips into the Underworld, like Eurydice.

I think of his mum and sisters and nephews and nieces back home, with nothing now to fuel their futures. Take the gold cross from around his neck and wrap it up in as many pound notes as I can spare. Post it back to them with a letter about how kind he was. Ask if I can keep his books.

At his wake everyone drinks too much, and they gang up on the union rep; push him deep into a corner, fingers poking at his chest: What's the union doing besides nothing? What about the shaft holes? When will they fix the broken housing?

I swallow down my fear, and shout at them to STOP!

What would Quinn think, you all at each other like this?! This is what they want, for us to be divided! We need to rally, to stay unified!

I feel powerful. Like I'm channelling Quinn. Like he's giving me strength.

DOT: She's right! Pull yourselves together, you lot!

PEARL: We need to make a plan. Someone needs to go to Kalgoorlie. Ask the hospital some questions about this place. Ask about the asbestos, why there's so much sickness here.

Beat.

Pasquale? You offering? Terrific. Take Angelo with you. Go to the library, as well. See what you can find.

Mick, as union rep you need to follow up on the protective gear, the shaft holes, extraction fans, housing conditions …

DOT: … they all start going for Mick again …

PEARL: No! Stop! It's not just his job. You *all* need to step up.

DOT: … that's my girl …

PEARL: They can't sack the lot of you; we need to do it together.

DOT: … never been prouder …

PEARL: We've taken enough shit.

DOT: … chip off the ol' block …

PEARL: They bury Quinn in the dry rocky graveyard, and I can't stop crying; thinking of him out here all alone forever, when everyone he loves is so far away.

I plant a ghost gum seedling dug up from the gorge and water it every day, but the brutal sun withers and kills it before the week is out.

A bird falls from the sky and lands at my feet. Perfectly intact, just— roasted.

… everything out here dies …

Feels like the world is shifting. Like there's whispering on the wind. Like the trees are bending with sorrow and the mountains are shrinking, drooping from the weight of the holes blasted into them. Sinking from the tonnes of tailings poured on top of them. Like this land was sacred, once, and now it just feels—
Used up. And spat out. And …

… broken …

Beat.

DOT: I want to go back there.

PEARL: It's a ghost town, Mum. There's nothing left. No electricity, no shops, no supplies. The pub's razed to the ground. Houses demolished. Hospital, school, cinema. All gone.

DOT: The sky will still be there. The wattle. The gorge. The ranges. The—

PEARL: It's devastated country, now. Full of poison.

DOT: It's where I felt fully alive.

PEARL: Well you'll be finding your own way back, coz I'm not going.

DOT: You loved it there.

PEARL: No, Mum. *You* loved it. Dragged me all the way out to the arse-end of nowhere because you wanted a wild ride into the outback: sun on your face, wind at your back, like being in your very own western. Drag the kid with you. Leave her to forage in the asbestos-lined wilderness while you go off—

DOT: How could I have known?

PEARL: —shagging some random—

DOT: They hid everything from us!

PEARL: You could have pulled your head out of the bloody sand! They knew about asbestos—knew it was poison before they even *built* the town. How could you not have known? All you had to do was ask.

DOT: You were there too!

PEARL: I was a kid!

> *Beat.*

DOT: I'm sorry, love. I thought I was taking you to a safe place. We had our own house, for the first time ever. We had community. Jobs. More money than we could—

PEARL: The Banyjima didn't get a house or a big fat wage. Just a humpy outside the perimeter. Not even allowed to come into town, except on race days. Didn't see you objecting to that.

DOT: It was a different time, Pearl.

PEARL: Not good enough, Mum. No-one's doing anything to clean it up. Not the government, and certainly not the company.

DOT: Things worked differently then.

PEARL: I'm talking about *now*! It's all still there! There's another mob back there now, lodging plans for a new mine. Right next to Karinjini. If that gets approved thousands of hectares of native bush will be decimated!

DOT: —why're you—

PEARL: —just to build another bloody—

DOT: —I don't—

PEARL: Understand! I want you to—

DOT: —I don't—

PEARL: —understand! That it's the same greed, the same—

DOT: —I'm not—

PEARL: —the same lack of principles, the same abdication of—

DOT: —it's not my fault!

PEARL: —responsibility, the same—

> DOT *hacks up her lungs.*

—Rio Tinto. Juukan Gorge. Forty-five—

> DOT *hacks even louder.*

—thousand years of—

> DOT *drowns* PEARL *out.*

—culture, blown into—

> DOT *suddenly stills.*

> *Beat.*

—cosmic dust.

> *A long pause.*

We need to talk about you going into palliative care.

DOT: What? Why?

PEARL: Because I …

> … I can't …

> I can't give you the care you need. That you're going to need.
> When you—

> when the—

> … it's …

> *Beat.*

They have the care facilities. I don't.

> *Beat.*

I can't do this any more. It's too—

> *Beat.*

I just—

> *Beat.*

I can't—

DOT: Are you punishing me? For taking you there?

PEARL: No! Jesus, I—

> *Beat.*

No.

Beat.

DOT: A whirlpool of regret whorls beneath me, churning deep.
Scoops me up. Spins me around. Swallows me whole.

… but you can't undo time, can you?

… you can't undo that …

Beat.

PEARL: The fellas come back from Kalgoorlie and call a meeting at the
pub. Tell us what they learned about this asbestosis; tell us about a
new disease called mesothelioma.

DOT: Brutal.

PEARL: Caused by the fibres.

DOT: Painful.

PEARL: Lodged deep in lung.

DOT: Swift.

PEARL: Playground, racetrack, airstrip—all coated with it.

DOT: They knew, all along.

PEARL: Those visiting doctors filed report after report. To management.
To the Government Chemical Laboratories.

DOT: They knew the asbestos was deadly.

PEARL: To the Inspector of Mines.

DOT: Knew the counts were through the roof.

PEARL: The Undersecretary for Mines.

DOT: Knew we were all working towards our own deaths.

PEARL: The Commissioner for Public Health.

DOT: All those reports, swept under the carpet.

PEARL: Government relies on taxes from these mines.

DOT: Bastards. We've been had. Lied to.

PEARL: Poisoned for their profits.

Beat.

DOT: The trolley lady comes around. Best part of the day. Grin and
tonic? she says.

She pours me a double, the volunteer. Not like it's going to kill
ya, she jokes

… every time …
She lights up a fag, leans against the trolley.
Grabs herself a wee nip before she moves on.
They say she takes a wee nip at every stop; ends up pissed as a parrot,
    zig-zagging her drinks trolley far into the night.

I sit outside and sip my drink,
    watch day weave itself into wreath of night.

Outside my room a tiny nest: thin, and twig-like
    strung tenuous between two branches;
    hovering in the space between worlds—frail, yet full of life.
    Two scrawny chicks, sweaty necks extended
    downy-soft, bobbing beaks
    eyes half-open, bulging for food. Bulging for life.

Listen to the trees breathe
    in—
    and out.

Nature never sleeps
    never dies
    never gives up.

Golden lift of sunset tips into twilight
    as day tilts itself towards night.
    Watch the giant orb of setting sun
    steal
    another day
    away
    from me.
    Beat.

PEARL: Rumours fly hot as the winds: the mine is in the red. Transport and labour costs are too high. Talks of closure and ruin.
DOT: Pearl sits me down at the kitchen table.
PEARL: I'm leaving.
DOT: Where to?

PEARL: Anywhere's better than this.

DOT: Feel pressure in my chest, like—
A fist, squeezing. Tight. Grab for breath, but—

PEARL: Do you want to come?

DOT: —and I can't stop crying; this—
torn feeling. Deep down inside me. A sadness. Dark, and heavy.
My home. This is my home. My Shangri-La. The friends I have
made here. The joy I have found.
… but even I feel it slipping away now; down the darkness of
the stopes, washed away by the rains. Faded by heat, and lies, and
disappointment.

PEARL: We bundle only what clothes and bits we need, leave the rest
behind. Quinn's books stay to be buried under the thickening dust
of a dying town.

DOT: Unless you can pay the airfare, the only way out of this place is
on the asbestos trucks.

PEARL: Luckily Mum's 'slept' with the truck driver. Several times.

DOT: Give him a wink. Hitch ourselves up. Prop on top of the hessian
sacks, stuffed with raw asbestos.

PEARL: Grind and crank and bump along the rocky, dusty road out to
Point Samson, trail of blue death hanging solid in the air behind us.

DOT: Bloke next to us hacks up his lungs and spits out clots of blood
over the side. He's skinny, and drawn, and yellow around the edges;
so I smile at him to give him some hope—but we both know there
isn't any.

PEARL: We get out at Point Samson, dump our things onto the sand, run
into the ocean.

DOT: Feel the freedom of endless clean all around us. Washwashwash
the poison from our bodies.

PEARL: Watch it leach away to mingle into the azure waves, draining
away the shadows of our past.

Beat.

I don't tell her. Can't tell her.
… that I have it too …
Here.
And here.

And here.
A shadow.
Blue, like hers.
Spread, like hers.
A live-wired grenade, lodged deep inside me.
One single, tiny fibre stuck in the lining of my lung, silently brewing; suddenly activated:
tick
tick
tick
and then you just count down to the inevitable:
six
five
four
three
two
one

zero.

You don't even get years. Just months.

Beat.

It's not the fear of dying that grips you in the blue neon light of dawn. It's the fear of never having lived.

Long beat.

DOT: The mine goes broke, and they just—
walk away.
PEARL: Leaving behind giant blue glaciers, like a lunar landscape so vast, you can see them from space.
DOT: … all those beautiful young men, sent home to die …
PEARL: Government stays silent as sloths.
DOT: No money to be made in cleaning up, is there?
PEARL: That glorious Banyjima country, defiled. Countrymen can't tend to their own lands safely any more. Ancient culture buried under three million tonnes of asbestos tailings: tiny, microscopic fibres, smaller than a grain of flour, just lying in wait

> to activate.
> Blowing across those lands in the hot Pilbara winds.

Beat.

DOT: Evening descends lonesome as a cowboy:

PEARL: Washing into the deep cool waters of the gorge.

DOT: wail of curlew, jagged and empty

PEARL: Hanging from the giant ghost gums in poisoned cobwebbed sheets.

DOT: howl of dingo, seeking its mate

PEARL: A landscape forever altered.

DOT: squeal of fruit bat

PEARL: A people lied to.

DOT: scurry of rat.

PEARL: A town deserted—left emptied, and grieving.
> Wittenoom is struck off the map. Degazetted.
> As if you can undo history, just by unnaming a town.

DOT: Doped up to the eyeballs, world in fog:
> endone
> temazepam
> tramadol
> morphine.

> Feel myself shred
> dwindle
> shrink
> recede.

> Hear a tiny voice whisper deep inside my skull:
> Was that it?

PEARL: What is the collective noun for grief?

DOT: Was that a life?

PEARL: A gullet

DOT: Light like sunshine slides into the room.

PEARL: A gape

DOT: My shiny Pearl, bringing me a sprig of wattle.

PEARL: A grievance

DOT: Each little flower like a tiny sun, exploding.

PEARL: … a given …

    Beat.

DOT: Blue skies and spinifex.
PEARL: What, Mum?
DOT: Ghost gums and budgies.
PEARL: The dogs of the apocalypse stand, hackles raised.
DOT: I loved you so much, it hurt me.
PEARL: Muzzles curved up towards the full, bright moon.
DOT: Here.
PEARL: Shudder of soul eclipsing—
DOT: And here.
PEARL: atoms reforming: soft, like stardust
DOT: And here.
PEARL: All the stars falling
DOT: My daughter.
PEARL: cold into the sea.
DOT: My shiny little Pearl.

    DOT *starts to dance, joyous and unfettered; spinning into a whirling blue cloud of hope.*

    She puts her hand out to PEARL *to join her.*

    PEARL *takes* DOT*'s hand and they dance together, abandoned and free.*

    It builds into the Dance of Life, ramped up as if it's the last one, ever.

    … and maybe it is …

THE END

RED STITCH | THE ACTORS' THEATRE

presents

Wittenoom

26 JANUARY – 19 FEBRUARY, 2023

Playwright
Mary Anne Butler

Director
Susie Dee

Set and Costume Design
Dann Barber

Lighting Design
Rachel Burke

Sound Design
Ian Moorhead

Stage Manager
Cassandra Fumi

Deputy Stage Manager
Georgina Bright

Assistant Lighting Design
Spencer Herd

Pearl – **Emily Goddard**
Dot – **Caroline Lee**

This play was developed through Red Stitch's INK writing program.

RED STITCH | THE ACTORS' THEATRE

Artistic Director
Ella Caldwell

General Manager
Fiona Symonds

Production Manager
David Bowyer

Front-of-House Manager
Penelope Thomson

Marketing Coordinator
Olivia Durst

Administrator
Cecelia Scarthy

RED STITCH ENSEMBLE

Ella Caldwell
Richard Cawthorne
Jing-Xuan Chan
Jessica Clarke
Kate Cole
Brett Cousins
Ngaire Dawn Fair
Daniel Frederikson
Emily Goddard
Kevin Hofbauer
Justin Hosking
Khisraw Jones-Shukoor
Darcy Kent
Caroline Lee

Chanella Macri
Olga Makeeva
Dion Mills
Georgina Naidu
Christina O'Neill
Joe Petruzzi
Dushan Philips
Tim Potter
Ben Prendergast
Kat Stewart
Sarah Sutherland
Andrea Swifte
David Whiteley
Harvey Zielinski

BOARD

Sophia Hall (Chair), Damon Healey (Treasurer), Henrietta Thomas (Secretary), Ella Caldwell, Catherine Cardinet, Humphrey Clegg, Andrew Domasevicius-Zilinskas, Belinda Locke, Michael Rich, and Sandra Willis.

We at Red Stitch acknowledge and pay our respects to Australia's First Peoples and Elders past and present, and offer our gratitude to the Boon Wurrung and Wurundjeri Woi Wurrung peoples of the Kulin Nation, on whose unceded lands we work.

THANK YOU

This development and production of *Wittenoom* would not have been possible without the generous support of our donors and partners

KINDRED DONORS

Andrew Domasevicius & Aida Tuciute
Carrillo Gantner AC & ZiYin Gantner AC
Jane & Stephen Hains & Portland House Foundation
The James Family Charitable Foundation
Maureen Wheeler AO & Tony Wheeler AO
Lyngala Foundation
Jane Hansen AO
Graham & Judy Hubbard
Graham Webster & Teri Snowdon
Beth Brown
Michal Alfasi
Per & Ingrid Carlsen
Anonymous
Brian Goddard in Memoriam
John Haasz
The Neff Family
Rosemary Walls
Larry Abel
Caitlin English
Linda Herd
Liz & Peter Jones
Michael Kingston
Alex Lewenberg
The Lewis Langbroek Charitable Trust
The Mothers
Jenny Schwarz
The Kate & Stephen Shelmerdine Family Foundation
Christina Turner
Anonymous

Anita & Graham Anderson
Michael Brindley & Karinn Altman
Diana Burleigh
Ella Caldwell
Elise Callander
Julie & Ian Cattlin
Anonymous
Edwina Mary Lampitt* in memoriam
John Field
Damon Healey
Barbara Long
Kate & Peter Marshall
Angela Matkovic
Pamela McLure
Kaylene O'Neill
Timothy Roman
Jenny Ryssenbeek
Simon Schofield
James Syme
Jane Thompson & Chris Coombs
Tony Ward & Gail Ryan
Ian & Grace Warner
Margaret & Peter Yuill

MAJOR PARTNERS

Restart Investment to Sustain and Expand (RISE) Fund – an Australian
Government initiative
Creative Victoria
City of Port Phillip
The Lionel & Yvonne Spencer Trust
Cybec Foundation
The Portland House Foundation
Lyngala Foundation
Playking Foundation
Malcolm Robertson Foundation
The Myer Foundation
Sidney Myer Fund

Rear 2 Chapel Street, St Kilda East, VIC 3183
http://redstitch.net/ | FB: @RedStitchTheatre | T: @redstitch
boxoffice@redstitch.net | 03 9533 8083

WRITER'S NOTE

Wittenoom the play wouldn't exist without a hugely fortuitous combination of people and factors: Susie Dee, Janine Baines and the Red Stitch INK program were crucial in supporting and encouraging me to find the story. An Australia Council Literature Board grant was pivotal in providing me time to write it. Actors Caroline Lee and Emily Goddard, composer and sound designer Ian Moorhead and Ella Caldwell joined Susie to form the development team behind the work, giving intelligent feedback to an early script which moved it forward in massive leaps.

...but in truth, it first started when I stalked Susie Dee at a PlayWriting Australia conference in Brisbane, in 2010 ...

It was my first conference as an attendee, and what stood out for me in the presented works was Susie's direction. The pieces she worked on were different, interesting, engaging in their interpretation. At the end of the conference, I plucked up the courage to ask if I could speak with her. She looked around the crowded room full of massive networking potential, nodded her head and gave me fifteen minutes of her full and undivided attention: every bit of her keen intelligence, intense curiosity and big heart focused on an unknown playwright in a massive act of professional and personal generosity. At the end of my stumbling 'pitch', she gave me her email address and told me to send her what I had. I walked away from that conference on a glowing cloud of hope.

I followed up via email, and unfortunately Susie couldn't do the dates for that project. Theatre being a long game, I remained hopeful that I would get to work with her at some time in the future. Flash forward to 2018. I met Susie for a coffee in Melbourne, and asked if she would consider directing my next play, *Broken*. *Broken* had already had two sold out Darwin Festival productions under the stunning direction of Gail Evans, and a Sydney season at Darlinghurst Theatre Company directed by Shannon Murphy in a powerful 'radio program' version, complete with radio mics and live foley on stage.

As a playwright, it's a great privilege to see your work re-imagined over time, and Susie Dee's fortyfivedownstairs production was riveting: sparse, evocative and enticing—drawing audiences deep into a world layered with surprising imagery; drawing in a stellar design team which made those bare boards rich with the imagery, sound and light of Australia's Central Desert. Between our Melbourne meeting and the production, Susie had made her own trip to Central Australia to experience first-hand the unique landscape and light where the play was set. She asked me to send her the research that had helped shape the play's world: images, articles, sound grabs, interviews—and then she captured this world with such absolute truth and integrity that it made me hungry to work with her again.

In 2019, Susie and I applied to the Red Stitch INK play development program as a writer/director team. Red Stitch accepted the proposal, and from there we hunkered down to create a new work together.

I fail often as a playwright. Either I start with an idea which I don't have the passion to live with for the three to five years it will take me to research and write the play, or my craft skills aren't yet quite up to the execution of possibilities which play around in my head so the wrack of self-doubt shipwrecks me and the work beyond rescue, or the idea/writing become trite and clichéd, and I end up hurling at against the wall.

The less said about my first drafts for the INK program, the better. Suffice to say they were hurled up against the wall, with Susie Dee's gentle encouragement. This is another reason that I love working with Susie. Her honesty and directness in feedback are cased inside such a massive heart and keen dramaturgical intelligence, that she urges me to push myself further in my craft; and the work is always the better for it.

For the INK play I tuned deeper into my gut, which held a story I'd been quelling for years. It was the story of my mother—Sally Butler—who died of lung cancer in 2001. I've never been able to write about her. It's been too close, too brutal. And now here she was, finally. Bubbling up inside me, demanding to have her story told.

Susie was due in Darwin in a fortnight, coming up for a few days development on a work I hadn't written yet, so I did what I call 'the vomit'—an intense and uncensored writing period where I let the words churn out of me without thinking about form, or structure, or character or storyline. I read a lot of poetry when I write, and during this 'vomit' period I came across the Barbara Kingsolver poem *Hope; An Owner's Manual* in which she says: 'Tiptoe past the dogs of the apocalypse that are sleeping in the shade of your future.' I saw my mum, dying of cancer, with two Dogs of the Apocalypse lying at her feet, waiting for her to die. This image started a flow of words which were—essentially—the recording of my mum's death, from her initial diagnosis to her end. I wrote this up as an uncensored seventeen-page monologue.

Susie arrived for our development and I handed her these pages. She took them into her room, emerged 30 minutes later, and said 'I love it. It's not a play yet. You know that, don't you. But we can definitely work with this.'

…we were on…

The next week I headed off on a trip to Broome, a research trip for my PhD in Literature; a novel and exegesis exploring the question: How do you write hope into the creative literature of the Anthropocene? I stopped off in Kununurra for a night with my friend Jo Roach—whose daughter Janine Baines was there. We listened to a Midnight Oil song, *Blue Sky Mine*, and Janine told me that this song was written about the blue asbestos mining town of Wittenoom, in WA's remote Pilbara region.

I'd never heard of Wittenoom, or blue asbestos. I was gobsmacked by what Janine told me, and ashamed that I'd never heard of the town before. John Gordon's Foreword in this publication offers up a deeply informed context of the history and ongoing issues resulting from this purpose-built town, so I won't repeat his vast and detailed knowledge here. But this town lodged in my gut, and I knew instantly that I'd found the other half of my play.

I completed my road trip and hunkered down in the Broome library for three days, researching Wittenoom. The characters of Dot—a single mother—and her daughter Pearl came to me through reading and listening to some of the stories told by Wittenoom's ex-residents. While informed by my research, and while facts found on public record are mentioned in the play, *Wittenoom* is a work of fiction; an imagining of what it would have been like to live and work out in the remote Pilbara in the early 1960s.

The play came out quickly after that road trip, shaping itself into a structure which jumped between the present—Dot's experience of mesothelioma (informed by my mum's cancer journey)—and the past; an imagined version of life in Wittenoom in the early 1960s. Another few days' development courtesy of Red Stitch with more intelligent interrogation by the development team tweaked the script until we felt it was ready to go.

That draft then won the Shane and Cathryn Brennan Prize for Playwriting, and I'm most grateful to the AWG and Shane and Cathryn Brennan for that opportunity.

Then Red Stitch programmed *Wittenoom* for 2023, and the amazing development team grew into a stellar production team under the helm of Susie Dee, welcoming Rachel Burke as lighting designer, Dann Barber on set and costume design, Cassandra Fumi as AD and stage manager, and Georgie Bright as assistant SM.

There are many people and organisations I would like to thank for this journey: Susie Dee, Ella Caldwell, Caroline Lee, Emily Goddard, Ian Morehead, Rachel Burke, Dann Barber, Janine Baines, Lyniece Bolitho, Tanya Heaslip, John Gordon, Gail Evans, Ciella Williams, Kelly Beneforti, Red Stitch Ensemble, Brown's Mart Arts, the Australia Council for the Arts, Michelle Broun, Jo Roach, Martin Pritchard, Robin Chappel and Angela Di Pasquale, whose PhD *Sistemazione and death: the role of the Wittenoom asbestos mine in the lives and deaths of Italian transnational workers* was a pivotal research document.

Thank you to all the organisations and individuals who support Literature in all its forms, and who support and advocate for the development of new Australian Theatre works.

Mary Anne Butler
Naarm (Melbourne),
December 2022

DIRECTOR'S NOTE

As a theatre director, I am always hungry and on the lookout for works that are bold, current and vibrant, works that resonate and are unafraid to tackle all corners of the Australian psyche.

I was lucky enough to meet Mary Anne Butler at a National Playwriting Festival many years ago in Brisbane. I remember her eyes, her directness and her liveliness.

But I was a director based in Melbourne and she, a playwright based in Darwin.

She contacted me a few years later, sending me her award-winning play *Broken*. Having read it, I was immediately taken with the characters, the poeticism and the vivid landscape she had managed to capture. We joined forces and pitched it to a couple of mainstage companies, but with no joy. Then, we were lucky to have Lab Kelpie, (a small independent company) pick it up and produce it at fortyfivedownstairs theatre in Melbourne in 2018.

Mary Anne joined us for rehearsals, and it was a joy to have her in the room—she was thoughtful, insightful and gracious, and we both knew this would be the start of an honest, dynamic working relationship.

We started a dialogue again in 2020, this time on a new work originally titled *Tiny Bones of Love* (part of Red Stitch Actors Theatre's INK Program), a work we both found ourselves struggling with. After a couple of early drafts and a flurry of emails and zooms I finally had the chance to visit Mary Anne in Darwin in 2021, where she showed me for the first time a new monologue that started like this:

The dogs of the apocalypse lie at her feet, ears alert.

...waiting...

They can feel it in their flesh-bones; under their fur

sense the rising of the soul into the night

as she floats, barely present;

not quite ready

to face the great emptiness.

I was immediately hooked, excited and curious to see where it could lead. Mary Anne was just about to depart in her campervan with her beauty of a dog, Chet, on a road (and research) trip from Darwin to Broome. Then, on this journey, she came across the story of a town in the Pilbara called Wittenoom—and its deadly legacy. She then saw how to frame and house this vivid story of death and dying.

In *Wittenoom*, the play, we see a

mother and her daughter move to a remote mining town where a joyous life and looming death dance side-by-side in the blue asbestos dust. Two narratives slowly unfold, one set in the past where life is in full swing and the other in the present, about a body that is diseased and dying. They are, first and foremost, stories about fecundity and the giving of life, but also of the taking of it and an awareness of time running out. They revolve around loss, love, memory, betrayal and grief and in them Mary Anne manages to capture 'humanity' in its most raw and fragile state.

In both *Broken* and *Wittenoom*, Mary Anne gives us a series of rich and multi-layered characters while also capturing the vast Australian outback, all in her typically spare, poetic style. Her writing, rich with imagery, visceral in its rendering, is also full of ideas that challenge and surprise. She has a gift for embedding humour and pathos into all of her plays, her wit sharp and bold and her heart ever present. For a director, all these elements are a gift, and in working on *Wittenoom* in preparation for its Red Stitch season, we had the luxury of having a short development with the two actors and composer present.

Hearing the voices come alive off the page gave Mary Anne the opportunity to rethink the structure of her script, which in turn brought a whole new dynamic to the work.

Mary Anne's writing is in so many ways potent, exemplary and courageous. She tackles and unpacks ideas head-on, with boldness, craft and gusto. She understands the demands of theatre in a way few writers do and working with her once again has been an absolute pleasure.

Susie Dee

MARY ANNE BUTLER
PLAYWRIGHT

Mary Anne Butler's plays have won the Victorian Prize for Literature, Victorian Premier's Drama Award, Shane and Cathryn Brennan Prize for Playwriting, a stage AWGIE and two NT Chief Minister's Book of the Year Awards. She's been nominated for the Griffin Theatre Award and twice for the Nick Enright Award (NSW Premier's Literary Awards). Mary Anne is a Sidney Myer Creative Fellow, Arts NT Fellow, Winston Churchill Fellow, Regional Arts Fellow and Asialink Fellow. She holds an MPhil in Creative Writing, MEd in Arts Education, and is undertaking a PhD in Literature, investigating how we write hope into the creative literature of the Anthropocene.

SUSIE DEE
DIRECTOR

Susie Dee has worked extensively in the theatre as a performer, deviser and director in Australia and overseas for the past 35 years. She has served as Artistic Director of three companies, Melbourne Workers Theatre (MWT), Union House Theatre (UHT) and Institute of Complex Entertainment (ICE), and created a number of large site-specific works with them. She has also directed works for MTC, Malthouse Theatre and many independent theatre companies and has been nominated for and won numerous awards, including the 2022 Australia Council Theatre Award. In 2019 she directed a double-bill of Patricia Cornelius' plays, SHIT and Love, which toured to the Venice Biennale Theatre Festival. This was followed in 2020 by Anthem, a large-scale, co-written work premiering at the Arts Centre Playhouse for the Melbourne Festival and going on to tour the Sydney and Perth Festivals. In 2021 she collaborated with Patricia Cornelius and Nicci Wilks on RUNT, which premiered at fortyfivedownstairs and was followed by two more seasons in Brisbane and Sydney. In 2022, Susie directed *The Amateurs* at Red Stitch Actors' Theatre.

DANN BARBER
SET AND COSTUME DESIGN

Dann Barber is an award-winning set and costume designer whose work is heavily influenced by his study of drawing and fine art at RMIT. He went on to be a graduate in design from NIDA. Recent work includes *Yentl* produced by Kadimah Yiddish Theatre at the Fairfax, Arts Centre Melbourne, 2022 and *The Amateurs* at Red Stitch Actors Theatre, 2022. Dann's work in musical theatre has seen him design for the Opera House, Drama Theatre, with *Rent* in 2021. Dann also designed *Barnum the Musical* at the Comedy Theatre in 2019 and *Chess* at the Regent Theatre in 2021. He was associate costume designer for Gabriela Tylesova for the Australian Ballet's *Sleeping Beauty* in 2016, choreographed by David Mcallister and again for Melbourne Theatre Company's *Shakespeare in Love* in 2019, directed by Simon Phillips. His work extends to film, working with Micheal Hili on a range of video clips for artists Flume, Mark Pritchard and Thom York. Dann has won Green Room awards for best design in cabaret for his set and costumes in *The Ghetto Cabaret* at fortyfivedownstairs, in 2019 and the best independent set and costume design for *The Mermaid* at La Mama in 2021. He is a regular guest lecturer at VCA and Melbourne University in model making and rendering techniques.

RACHEL BURKE
LIGHTING DESIGN

Rachel Burke has an extensive and highly awarded body of work over three decades for mainstage companies, independent theatre and architectural lighting design both nationally and internationally. Industry acknowledgment includes ten Green Room Awards for Theatre Lighting Design, IES Victorian and National Awards of Excellence for Lighting Design in 2005, 2010 and 2019 and Helpmann Award nominations in 2005 and 2015. Recent work includes a return season of Ash Flanders in *End Of.* for Griffin Theatre Company and *Gene Tree: Listen. Now. Again* for St Martins/RBGV and the transfer of *Sexual Misconduct of the Middle Classes* from MTC to Belvoir Theatre.

IAN MOORHEAD
SOUND DESIGN

Ian Moorhead is a Melbourne-based artist specialising in music composition and sound design for theatre, dance, film and radio. He has performed around Australia and internationally, including New York, London, Edinburgh, Dublin, Wellington, Calgary and Vancouver. He has worked with numerous companies, including Melbourne Theatre Company, Malthouse Theatre, State Theatre Company of South Australia, New Working Group, Back to Back Theatre, Red Stitch Actors' Theatre, Dee and Cornelius, Windmill Theatre Co, Barking Gecko, Lab Kelpie, La Mama, Leigh Warren and Dancers, Patch Theatre Company, Restless Dance Theatre, Vitalstatistix, Circus Monoxide, NICA, Arts Centre Melbourne, Radiophrenia, Wave Farm, Ten Days on the Island, the Australian Festival for Young People, Underbelly Arts Festival, FOLA, Big West Festival, Museum Victoria, the Australian Museum and ABC Radio. He has been nominated for two Green

Room Awards for his designs for *Jurassica* (Red Stitch Actors' Theatre in 2016) and *Looking Glass* (New Working Group in 2018).

CASSANDRA FUMI
STAGE MANAGER / ASSISTANT DIRECTOR

Cassandra Fumi is a stage manager and director. Recent credits include *Angels in America* (fortyfivedownstairs), *The Book of Exodus* (Fraught Outfit) and THE RABBLE (*YES, UNWOMAN, LONE, WAKE*). Cassandra has worked with Susie Dee as a stage manager on *Broken, Anthem, Archimedes War* (not final season). Cassandra has worked as a stage manager and show director on Samara Hersch's and Lara Thoms' *We All Know What's Happening* (Campbeltown Arts, Vitalstatistix, Zurich Theater Spectacle and Noorderzon Performing Arts Festival Groningen). She is the Associate Artist on *Body of Knowledge* with Samara Hersch 2019–2022. Their recent collaboration *It's Going To Get Dark* is part of Hyperlocal and will premiere in Europe in 2023. Cassandra's directing credits include; *The Mermaid* (La Mama Theatre, Green Room Award Winner for Design and Lighting—Independent), *DOG SHOW* (Melbourne Fringe, Winner Best Theatre Ensemble), *The Places You'll Go* (Adelaide Fringe, Winner Best Theatre) and *NADJA* (Cockpit Theatre, London). This is Cassandra's first production with Red Stitch. She is very excited to be working with this amazing team. www.cassandrafumi.com

GEORGINA BRIGHT
DEPUTY STAGE MANAGER

Georgina Bright is an emerging Melbourne-based arts manager and all-round theatremaker who has graduated from Monash University with a Bachelor of Arts and is completing her Master of Arts and Cultural Management at the University of Melbourne. Her most recent credits include various forms of management for *Ramona Glasgow* (Gasworks Art Park), *The Amateurs* (Red Stitch), *Archimedes War* (Darebin Arts), *Thank You for Calling* (Melbourne Fringe) and *The Love of the Nightingale* (Theatre Works). She has worked as the Keynote Intern for Melbourne Fringe and has worked as a collaborating artist for *We Are AIR* (Melbourne Fringe/CTP), *UnderEden Walkman* (Melbourne Fringe/STRANGEkit), *My Brilliant Career* (CTP), *The Bacchae* (La Mama) and *Slaughterhouse Five* (Theatre Works).

SPENCER HERD
ASSISTANT LIGHTING DESIGN

Spencer (he/him) is a lighting designer and technician with a keen eye for detail and nuance, working across all forms of live performance, including theatre, concerts and events, and nightclubs. Spencer's deepest passions for design are in the world of sound, whether that is music, composition, a soundscape or musical theatre. Graduating from WAAPA (Bachelor of Performing Arts: Production and Design, specialising in Lighting, 2018), he hopes to bring a new and innovative outlook into the industry as a collaborative and dynamic artist through new Australian works, queer stories and important voices. Spencer's recent credits include *Medea: Out of the Mouths of Babes* (Theatre Works), *Pull the Pin* (Blue Room Theatre), *A Hundred Words for Snow* (Theatre Works Explosives Factory), *Daddy* (Chillout Festival), *From All Who Came Before* (La Mama HQ) *Run and Bottom* (Gasworks Arts Park/Bluestone Church Arts Space). Spencer has also seconded with Trent Suidgeest on *Muriel's Wedding the Musical* for Global Creatures at Her Majesty's Theatre.

EMILY GODDARD
PEARL

Emily Goddard is an award-winning actor, writer and theatremaker. She graduated from Ecole Philippe Gaulier, Paris in 2010, supported by the Ian Potter Cultural Trust and Empire Theatres Bursary. Recent theatre credits include: *The Amateurs*, *Lamb*, *You Got Older* and *Glory Dazed* (Red Stitch), *Wayside Bride* and *Light Shining in Buckinghamshire* (Belvoir St), *Australian Realness* (Malthouse), *Noises Off*, *The Boy at The Edge of Everything* and *Elling* (MTC), *Angels in America* and *The Lonely Wolf* (Dirty Pretty Theatre), *Hamlet* (ASC), *Inner Voices* (Red Line/Old Fitz), *Mess* (The Bush, London/UK tour), *The Unspoken Word is Joe* (Brisbane Festival/MKA), *Moth* (Arena), *The Walls* (Attic/Erratic) and *Os Pequenos Nadas* (Ultimo Comboio Teatro, Barcelona). Emily's screen credits include *Clickbait*, *Ms Fisher's Modern Murder Mysteries*, *Neighbours*, *Newton's Law* and *Twentysomething*. Her critically acclaimed play *This is Eden* was winner of the 2018 Drama Victoria Award and has had six sell-out seasons, including a recent Australian tour. Emily has been nominated for three Green Room Awards for Outstanding Female Actor, most recently for *This is Eden*. She is currently completing her Masters of Screenwriting at the VCA and developing an original dramedy series *All There Is* with Ruby Entertainment.

CAROLINE LEE
DOT

Caroline Lee is based in Melbourne, Australia, and has worked professionally as a theatre, television, film and voice actress for over 30 years. She has worked with the Malthouse, Sydney Theatre Company, Melbourne Theatre Company, Bell Shakespeare, Back to Back Theatre, Red Stitch Actors Theatre, Chamber Made Opera, MKA, Finucane and Smith, HeLD Productions, Hildegard, Playbox and La Mama, as well as developing a strong reputation for her work in one-woman shows. Caroline has received four Green Room Awards and an OAM for her work in the theatre. Caroline has narrated over 150 audiobooks, including a number of best-selling titles, including *Big Little Lies* and *Truly Madly Guilty* by Liane Moriarty, and *The Shifting Fog* and *The Forgotten Garden* by Kate Morton. She has received three AudioFile Earphones Awards, including Best Audiobook of the Year 2021 for *Apples Never Fall* by Liane Moriarty. Film and television appearances include a supporting cast role in *The Newsreader* and *The Newsreader 2*, a main cast role in *Bogan Pride*, and roles in *Miss Fisher's Modern Murder Mysteries*, *The Dressmaker*, *Tangle*, *Winners and Losers*, *Satisfaction*, *Stingers*, *MDA*, *Halifax fp*, *Blue Heelers*, *Neighbours*, *Holidays on the River Yarra* and *Dogs in Space*, as well as a number of smaller film projects with independent producers.

RED STITCH ACTORS' THEATRE

We are an actor-led ensemble, enriching our community by empowering artists as cultural leaders. We inspire audiences with compelling contemporary theatre that engages with the complexities of humanity and reveals us to ourselves. Our organisational model nurtures artistic vibrancy and growth.

Red Stitch is a creative hub, offering scope for artists to make work they are passionate about in a sector where such opportunities are limited. As the ensemble and executives of Red Stitch, we provide a platform where leading practitioners can hone their craft and take risks, and emerging artists can work alongside mid-career and seasoned professionals. We play a vital role in the development and presentation of new Australian works through our INK playwriting program, promoting local voices alongside acclaimed contemporary international work which may not otherwise be seen by local audiences.

www.redstitch.net

Red Stitch would like to thank the following supporters who generously contribute to our INK program.

Australian Government
RISE Fund

CREATIVE VICTORIA

CITY OF PORT PHILLIP

Cybec
Foundation

MALCOLM ROBERTSON FOUNDATION

THE PORTLAND HOUSE FOUNDATION

PLAYKING
FOUNDATION

Lyngala
Foundation

THE MYER
FOUNDATION

SIDNEY MYER FUND

Kindred